TEEN LIFE™

FREQUENTLY ASKED QUESTIONS ABOUT

Kidnapping and Abduction

Randy Shattuck
and
Kristina Lundblad

ROSEN
PUBLISHING®

New York

Published in 2012 by The Rosen Publishing Group, Inc.
29 East 21st Street, New York, NY 10010

Library of Congress Cataloging-in-Publication Data

Shattuck, Randy.
Frequently asked questions about kidnapping and
abduction/Randy Shattuck, Kristina Lundblad.—1st ed.
    p. cm.—(FAQ: teen life)
Includes bibliographical references and index.
ISBN 978-1-4488-5563-6 (library binding)
1. Kidnapping. 2. Abduction. I. Lundblad, Kristina. II. Title.
HV6595.S48 2012
364.15'4—dc23

                                                        2011018765

Manufactured in China

CPSIA Compliance Information: Batch #W12YA: For further information, contact Rosen Publishing, New York, New
York, at 1-800-237-9932.

Contents

1 What Are the Types of Kidnapping and Abduction? 4

2 How Do Kidnappers Operate? 14

3 What Are Some Ways to Stay Safe at Home? 23

4 What Are Some Safety Tips for Being in Public Places? 30

5 How Can You Use the Internet Safely? 45

6 What Is Society Doing About Abduction? 50

Glossary 55
For More Information 56
For Further Reading 60
Index 62

one

WHAT ARE THE TYPES OF KIDNAPPING AND ABDUCTION?

Every day, news reports show how vulnerable children and teenagers are to kidnapping, also known as abduction. Kidnapping is the taking of a person using physical force, threats, or tricks. It is a serious and dangerous problem. According to the *Juvenile Offenders and Victims 2006 National Report*, one-third of all kidnap victims known to law enforcement are under the age of eighteen. Some are sexually abused, some are later found murdered, and some are never seen again.

As reported by the U.S. Department of Justice (DOJ), it is estimated that every year more than 258,000 children and teens are abducted in the United States. Reported statistics of abductions are often considered only estimates. The lack of a more concrete number is a reflection of the reality that not all abduction cases are reported to law enforcement. Also, when a child

18:21:41 02/01/2004

In 2004, a man is captured on video abducting eleven-year-old Carlie Brucia in Sarasota, Florida. Brucia was returning home from a sleepover and was taking a shortcut near her home. She was found murdered.

is abducted and later found dead, the police often classify the crime as a murder instead of an abduction. Similarly, the crimes of abduction and rape may be classified only as a rape. The actual number of abductions, then, is higher than the official numbers indicate.

There are various safety precautions that you can take to protect yourself and others from being abducted from home, in public places, and from contacts made online. It is also useful to learn who abductors are (statistics show that the vast majority are men), how they choose their victims, what tricks they use to lure young people into dangerous situations, and how to tell the difference between a safe stranger and a dangerous stranger. Kidnappings by strangers or nonfamily members may be the most feared form of abductions; however, abductions by loved ones are quite common.

Nonfamily Abductions

According to the DOJ, a nonfamily abduction happens when a person takes an unrelated child by physical force or threat of bodily harm and keeps that child for at least an hour in a secluded place without legal authority or parental permission. A nonfamily abduction also occurs when a child who is younger than fifteen or is mentally incompetent, without legal authority or parental permission, is taken or held by or willingly accompanies a nonfamily perpetrator who conceals that young person's location, demands ransom, or reveals the intention to keep the young person permanently. Nonfamily abductions include those that are known as stereotypical kidnappings. A nonfamily abductor or kidnapper can be an acquaintance, neighbor, long-term friend of the family, babysitter, or stranger.

The Second National Incidence Studies of Missing, Abducted, Runaway, and Thrownaway Children (NISMART–2) were conducted from 1997 to 1999, with the majority of the data concentrated in 1999. Published by the DOJ in October 2002, the NISMART-2 data are currently still considered by many author-

This billboard in Salt Lake City, Utah, publicized the kidnapping of fourteen-year-old Elizabeth Smart, who was abducted from her bedroom by knifepoint in 2002. Smart was found alive about nine months later, after being repeatedly molested by her captors.

ities to be the most accurate. NISMART–2 found that 58,200 children were victims of nonfamily abductions in 1999.

NISMART–2 defines stereotypical kidnapping as "a nonfamily abduction perpetrated by a slight acquaintance or stranger in which a child is detained overnight, transported at least 50 miles (80.5 kilometers), held for ransom or abducted with intent to keep the child permanently, or killed." Nearly half of the child victims of stereotypical kidnapping or nonfamily abductions were sexually assaulted by the perpetrator. Girls were the predominant victims of both nonfamily abductions and stereotypical kidnapping.

Pedophiles

Having sex with children or young people under the age of eighteen is illegal in the United States. Police statistics show that most nonfamily abductors are child molesters, adults who engage in sexual activities with children or young people. Child molesters are also called pedophiles. They prey on both boys and girls.

Some child molesters have been previously convicted of raping or sexually molesting children or young people. Many of these criminals are free on the streets. This is because, even when they are caught, they often serve relatively short prison terms before being released. According to the DOJ, there are roughly five hundred thousand registered sex offenders in the United States. Studies show that many child molesters who have been caught, jailed, and treated will probably return to child molesting once they are released from prison.

Child Pornography

Child pornography is sometimes a motive for abduction. Some perpetrators abduct children to photograph or videotape them in sexual situations. The possession and distribution of child pornography is illegal under federal law, laws in all fifty states, and in many other countries. However, there is an underground market for such material among pedophiles throughout the world.

Law enforcement officials believe child pornography is increasing due to the growing use of the Internet. The illegal images used in child pornography can be presented in print, videotape, CDs, and DVDs. The images can then be transmitted online through the use of bulletin boards, news groups, chat rooms, social networking sites, and e-mail.

Family Abductions

Every year, about 1.3 million children are reported missing in the United States. Most of these young people have simply gotten lost or have run away, are found quickly, and are returned home unharmed.

According to NISMART-2, of the 1.3 million cases of missing children, 203,900 involved abductions by family members, such as a parent. The children are often taken across state lines to prevent others from finding them. Although parents who abduct their own children are breaking the law, they often don't harm their children. They simply want their children to live with them. Three-fourths of the children who are abducted are young adolescents (between the ages of twelve and fourteen) and older teenagers (between the ages of fifteen and seventeen).

Runaways and Kidnapping

Other missing young people are runaways. There are as many as 1.7 million young people in the United States who run away from their homes every year, according to DOJ statistics. Runaways leave home when family troubles become too difficult for them to handle. Most runaways, however, return home after a few days. Runaways are especially in danger of abduction because they often live on the streets, and there is no one to protect them. They can be robbed, raped, forced into prostitution, become a victim of human trafficking, or even murdered.

Multiple Crimes

Abduction is often only the first step in a series of crimes. Abductors want to get their victims alone. They will use force, tricks, or bribery to lure their victims to go with them. Rapists often abduct their victims and take them to secluded places where there will be no witnesses to the attacks. Many serial killers abduct their victims before murdering them. Protecting yourself from abduction will protect you from other crimes as well.

Long-term Effects

Abduction is a serious problem that has taken the lives of many young people. Sometimes, abducted children are sexually

A call center supervisor at the National Runaway Switchboard helps homeless and runaway youths through crisis intervention and referrals to local services and resources.

assaulted and then released. These children and their families and friends are sometimes able to heal and return to normal lives. However, more often than not, the experience will have lasting, often devastating, effects on the rest of their lives.

You can help protect yourself, your friends, and your siblings from abduction by taking the necessary precautions with your friends and with children you know. The more young people know about the crime of abduction and how to protect themselves, the better their chances are of not becoming victims.

Myths and Facts

It's OK to hitchhike if you are with more than one person. Fact: ➤ It is never OK to hitchhike. Even if you are with a friend, putting yourself alone in a car with a stranger is just too dangerous. If the driver has a weapon, he can easily overpower both of you. Find another mode of transportation.

Most children who are abducted are taken by strangers. Fact: ➤ Most child victims of abduction are not taken by strangers. According to the Office of Juvenile Justice and Delinquency Prevention's *The Crime of Family Abduction: A Child's and Parent's Perspective*, May 2010, more than two hundred thousand children become victims of family abduction; nearly fifty-eight thousand children were victims of nonfamily abduction.

To avoid abduction, it is much safer to drive than walk.

Fact: ➡ Just because you are inside your vehicle doesn't make you safe from predators. Abductors can enter your car through an unlocked door. Be sure to keep all doors locked when sitting in your parked car and while driving. At night, be sure to park in a busy area close to a streetlight. To be extra cautious, do not drive alone at night. Have a friend escort you to your car.

HOW DO KIDNAPPERS OPERATE?

When you were younger, your parents probably taught you never to talk to strangers. Parents know that talking to the wrong sort of stranger can be dangerous. But even as you grow older and think you know how to tell the difference between a safe and a dangerous stranger, you can be deceived by tricks criminals use. Even adults are sometimes fooled by a friendly personality and a nice smile.

You talk to many people every day—store clerks, mail carriers, bank tellers, and others—who are strangers to you. Talking to strangers is necessary. You cannot get through a typical day without talking to strangers. But some strangers are dangerous, and they want to harm you. How do you tell the difference between normal and dangerous strangers? How do you avoid strangers who want to harm you?

One method abductors use to lure young people away is to ask for directions or for help in finding a pet.

How Dangerous Strangers Lure Young People

Normal strangers often talk to you in the course of doing their jobs. For example, the bus driver will talk about the traffic. Normal strangers usually exchange a few words and then go on their way. Dangerous strangers begin talking to you for no apparent reason or ask you inappropriate or personal questions. They may ask if you are alone, what is your name, or where you live. They may ask you to go somewhere with them. Normal strangers won't do this. Normal strangers won't try to engage you in a lengthy or personal conversation nor try to talk you into going somewhere with them.

Dangerous strangers will often look around while they are talking as if they don't want to be seen talking to you. Strangers who are worried about someone seeing the two of you together should be a warning sign that they may be dangerous.

Some people think that unsafe strangers will look dirty or crazy, but you should realize that a dangerous stranger will probably look like everyone else. A smile or a friendly face is not enough to make a stranger into a friend. People's behavior is what makes them dangerous, not their appearance.

Signs of Danger

You should be aware that friendly strangers may be the most dangerous. This is especially true for teen girls. Most abductors are men, and most victims are women, especially young women. According to the Rape, Abuse and Incest National Network, one in six American women has been the victim of an attempted or completed rape. Girls who are between the ages of sixteen and nineteen are four times more likely than the general population to be victims of rape, attempted rape, or sexual assault.

Teen girls may be tempted to talk with a stranger if he is good-looking and seems friendly. Many are fooled by a handsome, smiling man who seems to be flirting with them. They are flattered by his attention. You need to remember that it is a person's behavior that makes him dangerous, not his physical appearance. Any stranger who wants to be alone with you, who offers you a ride in his car, or who invites you to his house—no matter how friendly he may seem—may be a threat to your safety.

Part of protecting yourself and others against abduction involves knowing what tricks abductors frequently use to lure potential victims, who they typically target, and where they usually find their victims. Abductors have been using the same sorts of tricks, looking for similar kinds of victims, and abducting their victims in the same types of places for many years. Knowing how abductors operate can save you from becoming an abductor's next victim.

Kidnappers Ask for Help

One trick abductors use is to ask a young person for help. The abductor may ask for directions or for help with his car door because his arms are loaded with packages. Abductors may ask you to help them carry their groceries or help them find a lost pet. You should be suspicious of any stranger who asks for your help. When adults need help, they turn to other adults, not young people they do not know. Any stranger who asks for your help should be avoided.

They Offer Bribes

When you were younger, your parents and teachers probably taught you not to take candy from strangers. They know that

Another common ploy that kidnappers use to abduct young people is to tell them there is a crisis at home and that he or she has been sent by the family to take the young person to the hospital immediately.

abductors often use candy or other treats as a bribe to convince children that they are a friend. Just as small children should not accept candy from strangers, teenagers must not accept gifts from strangers. Abductors might bribe teenagers with drugs or alcohol, a chance to play a new computer or video game, or a ride to the mall. Some teenagers have been abducted by strangers who offered them jobs. Abductors know that a well-paying job is hard for some teens to turn down. Remember that real employers do not stop people in the street and offer them work. They run "Help Wanted" ads in newspapers or go through employment agencies to find employees.

If someone approaches you on the street and offers you something that sounds too good to be true, it probably is. You don't know the person, and he doesn't know you, so why would he do you such a favor? Ask yourself what other motives the person might have. Don't be fooled by a bribe.

There's a Family Emergency

Another common trick abductors use is to make up a story about a family emergency. This trick is often used on small children, but it's sometimes used on teenagers, too. For example, a stranger may approach you walking home from school and say, "Your mom's been in an accident, and she asked me to take you to the hospital right away." Or he may say, "I know your dad from work. He can't pick you up, so he sent me instead." It is important to know immediately that such stories sound wrong and that your parents would never send a stranger to drive you anywhere. Never believe any story a stranger tells you about an illness or an accident in the family. If there has been an emergency, your family will get in touch with you. They will not send a stranger.

They Pose as Someone Else

An abductor may pretend to be a police officer, a minister, a schoolteacher, or a utility person. Few children will think there is any danger in getting into a car with a police officer who has shown them a badge. You may think it is safe to help a man wearing a clerical collar find his lost keys. But keep in mind that a stranger wearing a uniform is still a stranger. Unless there is a good reason to think that someone is a real police officer or minister or other authority figure, it is safer to stay away. Look for clues before getting involved with the person. A man wearing a police uniform who steps out of a patrol car is probably a real police officer. A man who only shows you a badge may not be; he may be impersonating an officer.

Also, ask yourself if what the person is asking you to do falls under his job description. A real police officer wouldn't ask you to get into his car without a legitimate reason. A real minister wouldn't come up to a young person on the street and ask for help to find his lost keys. Examine the situation and use your best judgment. If you don't trust the person or what he says, or something doesn't feel right, don't get involved with him.

Younger children—such as your little brother or sister—often think that if someone knows his or her name, that person is not a stranger but a friend. Abductors know this and will try to trick a small child into telling his or her name. The abductor may call the child by the wrong name to get the child to say his or her correct name. The abductor may also read the name off a name tag on the child's clothing or overhear someone else say it. Young children need to be aware that just because someone knows their name doesn't mean that person should be trusted.

Abductors Might Use Physical Force

Although most abductors trick their victims into going with them, some will use force or threats instead. These abductors

A U.S. Marshal displays some confiscated fake badges. Some kidnappers impersonate law enforcement officials and wear fake badges to get a young person into a car or to a secluded spot.

will threaten the victim with a weapon, such as a knife or a gun. They may simply grab the person and pull them into a car or van. This kind of abduction will usually take place in a secluded area. Abductors do not want witnesses to their crime. They do not want anyone to hear their victim's cries for help.

Crying out for help is exactly the thing to do if you find yourself in such a situation. You become a more difficult target if you make noise. This is often the most common tip that police officers give to the public about defending against kidnappings. Abductors are often scared away when their intended victims make a lot of noise.

three

WHAT ARE SOME WAYS TO STAY SAFE AT HOME?

Taking safety precautions is especially important in the home. If an abductor gets inside your home, you will be in a confined space, where your cries for help will not be heard. Don't open your door to any stranger—no matter what story he tells you.

I'll Show You an ID!

Criminals have found that pretending to be someone official, such as a deliveryman, repairman, building inspector, or meter reader from a utility company, is a useful trick for getting inside a house. Fake repairmen may say that your neighbors have been having phone problems and they want to check your phone, too. Once inside the home, they abduct, rob, sexually assault, and murder innocent people.

Always ask to see an ID card from a deliveryman before opening the door, and look for a proper uniform. If something doesn't seem right, do not open the door.

Many of these crimes can be prevented with simple precautions. If someone claims to be from the post office or from a mail delivery company, look at the uniform. Does the jacket match the trousers? Do the shoes match the uniform? Many times, the criminal has stolen only part of a full uniform and the rest of his clothes do not match. Is there a mail truck or delivery truck parked nearby? Real postal employees delivering packages will do so in a truck; they will not walk door-to-door with an armload of packages. Look at the package, too. Is it addressed to you? Does it have a return address from someone you recognize? Are you expecting a package?

If you have any doubts about a postal employee at the door, just ask that he leave the package outside or tell him that you will pick it up at the post office later. It is better to go through some extra trouble over a package than to put yourself at risk for abduction, robbery, sexual assault, or even murder.

Repairmen who come to the door must also be checked carefully. If you are not expecting a repairman, do not let him in. Real repairmen do not arrive unannounced. If you have asked for a repairman, check his ID through the window (do not open the door!) or call his office before you let him in. See whether he has come in a marked company truck or van. You should be suspicious of any story a stranger at the door tells you. Just because a stranger is wearing a work uniform and carrying tools does not mean he is a real repairman. Also, be wary of people who say they are collecting signatures or donations for a political or charitable cause. Abductors posing as such may try to entice you to let them in or even just to open the door to hand them money or sign a form so that they can force their way in.

May I Use Your Phone?

A popular trick that criminals use to enter homes is to ask if they can use the telephone. They play on our natural desire to be polite and helpful. When a stranger says, "My car has broken down, and my cell phone is dead. May I use your phone to call a tow truck?" it is easy to say, "Yes." But knowing about this trick can prevent you from falling for it.

One good way to protect yourself from a potential abductor is to tell the person that you will make the phone call for him. If the stranger claims that there has been a car accident, offer to call the police. If someone is sick or hurt, offer to call an ambulance. Offering to make the call yourself—while the stranger waits outside—will defeat the trick. If there is a real problem and the stranger is telling the truth, you will help out by making the phone call for him. If it is a trick, however, you will keep the criminal from getting inside your house.

While You Are Babysitting

When you agree to babysit someone else's children, you must take the job seriously. You are temporarily assuming the role of a parent to the children you are caring for. Good babysitters take precautions to ensure that the children in their care are safe. Before the parents leave, ask who the children may play with, where the children may play, and who may visit while the parents are gone. Get the phone number and address of where the parents will be. Also, make sure that you have emergency phone

When you babysit for someone, always think about your and the children's safety. Know emergency phone numbers and where parents can be reached, if necessary. Secure the household so that strangers cannot get in.

numbers handy for the police, fire department, and the nearest hospital.

Lock the doors immediately after the parents leave. Do not let anyone into the house who has not been approved by the parents beforehand. If someone who has not been approved comes to the door, tell the person that you will deliver a message for him or her. Never allow the children to answer the door. If the phone rings, do not tell the caller that you are home alone with the children. Tell the caller that the parents are unavailable at the moment and take a message.

If the parents have told you that the children can play in the yard, watch the children closely when they are outside. Stay nearby to make sure they do not wander off. Be aware of anyone who is hanging around or trying to talk to you or the children. If a situation or person makes you feel uncomfortable, take the children inside immediately, lock the door, and call the police.

If you are babysitting at night, do not allow the children to go outside. If you hear strange noises or detect odd activity, don't go outside yourself. Instead, switch on the outside lights and call the police immediately.

Kidnappers sometimes follow their victims home. Always be aware of your surroundings, and if you've been driven home by a friend, make sure that he or she waits until you are inside before leaving.

Following You Home

Some abductors simply follow their victims home and force their way in when the victims have opened the front door. To prevent this, have your keys out and ready. Check that no one is behind you before opening your door. Also, try to attract the attention of others by making noise. Abductors often shy away from a potential victim when he or she makes a lot of noise.

If you are driven home, have the person wait until you are safely inside your home. When returning from a friend's house, always have your friend call to make sure you got home safely.

four

WHAT ARE SOME SAFETY TIPS FOR BEING IN PUBLIC PLACES?

Whenever you are in a public place, you are a potential crime victim. In public places, such as shopping malls or a baseball stadium, people meet and mingle with many strangers. Criminals look for victims wherever people ordinarily gather.

Being careful in public places means being aware of the people around you and what they are doing. You can avoid being the victim of a crime by avoiding the people and situations that may be dangerous to you.

In Parking Lots

Many crimes occur in the parking lots of stores and office buildings. Because of the many vehicles parked there, it is

Criminals can lurk in parking lots. Always have your keys ready, and once inside your car, quickly lock the doors and drive away. Never approach your vehicle if someone is loitering nearby.

often hard to spot a criminal in a parking lot. He can crouch between parked cars or hide behind a parked van. He can even wait in his own car for someone to approach. Criminals have stolen cars and robbed, sexually assaulted, abducted, and even murdered people in parking lots.

To protect yourself in a parking lot, be on the lookout for strangers who may be hanging around. Don't walk where you cannot easily be seen by others, such as behind a parked truck or van. At night, park under a streetlight. Park as close as you can to the store or building that you are going to visit. Park so that your door is not next to a van or truck. When you get out of the car, it is easy for someone in a van to grab you and pull you inside without anyone else noticing.

Before you get out of your vehicle, look around to see if there is anyone suspicious nearby. Do not get out if there is. Drive to another parking space if you do not feel safe where you are. When you get out of your car, unlock only the door you are using. Rapists and thieves sometimes jump into a car through the passenger side when the doors are unlocked.

When you walk from your car to the store, do not walk too closely to other parked cars. Criminals can hide between parked cars, especially at night. Walk in the middle of the lane, keeping as much space as possible between you and the cars.

When you return to your car, have your keys in your hand, ready to open the door. If you see a suspicious person hanging around your car, walk back to the store and report him to the security guard. Before getting into your parked car, check that no one is hiding in the backseat or on the floor.

If you are carrying packages from the store, take them inside the car with you. Do not stop to put them in the trunk. When you put packages in the trunk, you turn your back to people approaching, which makes it easy for someone to sneak up on you. If you have a large package, have a store employee help you carry it to your car or drive to the store entrance and load it into the trunk there.

If you are shopping in a mall, ask a security guard to walk you to your car. Many malls have such a courtesy patrol. It is best to finish your shopping before most of the other shoppers leave,

Young children often wander off in stores and thus are easy targets for abductors. If you have younger brothers or sisters, talk to them about staying close so that you can keep an eye on them while shopping.

so that there are plenty of other people around.

In Stores

Child molesters often go to stores to find young children. A molester looks for a child who is lost or whose parent or older brother or sister is not paying attention. The molester will then try to take the child from the store. Sometimes, he will tell the child a fake story to try to trick him or her into leaving. Other times, he will simply grab the child and drag him or her out of the store. Even if the child cries, most people won't think the child is being abducted. They may think that the child has misbehaved and is being punished or that the child is crying because he or she is not feeling well.

Teach your younger brothers and sisters that if they get lost at a store, they should not wander around looking for their parents. They should not leave the store. They should go to a store clerk at the cash register or to a uniformed security guard at the door. Going to a mother or father with children is also safe. The child should say that he or she is lost and needs help.

You can protect your younger brothers and sisters by watching them carefully when you are in a store together. Small children often get bored while their parents or older siblings are shopping. They are easily distracted by the merchandise on display or by playing a game of hide-and-seek to pass the time. When you are shopping, make sure that your younger brothers and sisters stay nearby.

A good way to do this is to involve them in the shopping process. Ask them to help you find the items you want to buy. As you walk along a store aisle, they can point and show you the item when they see it. Ask them what color or style they like best. Involving children in your shopping keeps them from getting distracted and separated from you.

Walking Down the Street

Most strangers grab their victims while walking down the street. If possible, do not walk alone. Have a friend walk with you. Avoid walking after dark. If you have to walk in the dark, walk only in well-lit areas. Keep away from shadowy walkways or places hidden by overgrown shrubbery. These are places where an attacker can hide. Keep yourself in view of others as much as possible. Do not take shortcuts through wooded areas or down alleys. These are isolated places where a crime can easily be committed against you without any witnesses.

If you notice someone following you on foot, cross the street or walk to a building or group of people. If the person following

While walking or jogging, make sure you stay away from wooded areas that are deserted. Walk with a friend or in a group where there are lots of people around so that you aren't an easy victim.

you is persistent, go into a store or gas station and ask the clerk to call the police. If a car follows you, walk in the opposite direction from the way the car is driving. This makes it harder for you to be followed. If someone gets out of the car and comes toward you, run into a store or other public place or toward a group of people. If you need to, scream to attract the attention of others in the area.

If the attacker drives away, try to get his license plate number, or try to remember what he looks like or what he was wearing. Immediately report it to the police. You may save someone else from being abducted. Abductors often try several possible victims before finding one they can easily attack.

Going Jogging and Bike Riding

Many young people enjoy jogging or bicycling for exercise or recreation. Although these activities can be healthy and fun, they can also be potentially dangerous, so always take precautions.

Many attacks on joggers or cyclists take place in isolated areas of parks or on scenic wooded trails where few people are around. It is safer to jog where you can always see and be seen by other people. Busy streets or crowded public parks with many pedestrians are the safest places for jogging or cycling.

Joggers should not run alone. Criminals often see a lone woman as a much easier target. It is much safer to run with a friend or two. Even running with your pet dog will increase your level of safety.

Always jog or cycle in the daytime. During daylight hours, criminals have less of a chance to attack or abduct you without being seen. If you have to run or cycle in the evening, do it in well-lit, well-populated areas.

If a car or van approaches while you are jogging or bicycling, move away from the street. Be especially suspicious of vans because you can be quickly pulled inside and out of sight. If the vehicle slows down or pulls up alongside you, run or cycle in the opposite direction from the way it is headed. Go to the nearest populated place—an office building or a gas station—and call the police. Try to give a description of the car or van, the driver, and the license plate number. This will help the police track him down faster.

Many joggers and cyclists carry a small handheld alarm to sound if they get into trouble. A loud noise will always draw attention to you, and no criminal wants to attract attention. Others carry defense sprays, such as Mace or pepper spray. Think carefully before buying such a spray, however, because an attacker could snatch it away and use it on you. These products should only be used as last resorts.

Be Aware of Your Surroundings

Forcible abduction can also be prevented by a strong, confident attitude. Abductors often choose victims who look like easy targets. They want someone who will go along with them quietly without resistance. If you are alert in public, keeping aware of who is nearby and what they are doing, you are a harder target

Kidnappers look for victims who aren't paying attention to their surroundings. If you are distracted by a cell phone or MP3 player, you might not hear someone approach.

for abductors. If you seem confused, lost, or distracted, you make yourself an easier target.

You and most of your friends probably have cell phones and/or MP3 players. It is easy to be distracted while using these pieces of equipment. Wearing headphones or talking on your cell phone, however, makes it easier for someone to take you by surprise. Convicted serial killers have told police that they chose their victims based on how they behaved in public. They have said that alert persons were too difficult to take by surprise, but inattentive people made easy targets. If you stay aware of your surroundings whenever you are in a public place, you greatly lessen your chances of being abducted.

If you do not have a cell phone, you may have to use a public telephone on the street. Some criminals prey on people using public telephones because the victims are turned away from the street and cannot see them approach. The victims' hands are busy holding the phone, fumbling with coins, or dialing the number.

To reduce the risk of abduction while using a pay telephone, choose a phone located in a populated area and be sure it can be seen from the street. Make sure that there are no parked trucks or vans blocking your view. Pay attention to your surroundings, even as you insert the coins into the phone and dial the number. And then be sure to face the street while you are talking on the phone.

Remember to Make Noise!

If someone tries to abduct you, remember that he does not want to attract attention to himself. Anything you can do to attract the attention of other people will make him want to leave you alone. In previous attempted abduction cases, small children who were helpless in fighting off their abductors have screamed so loudly that they caught the attention of nearby persons who came and stopped the abduction.

If you make noise, you become a difficult target. You may attract the help of people in the vicinity. Shouting for help or making any sort of loud noise can scare an abductor away.

Use Code Words

Child protection experts recommend that parents or guardians arrange a secret code or password with their children. If someone approaches you on the street and tells you that your parents sent him, ask the person for the password. If the person doesn't know it, you will know that your parents didn't send him, and you should get away from this person as quickly as possible.

Carjackings

Carjacking, the theft of a car through the use of force or threats against the driver, is a growing problem in the United States. It is a serious crime in which the victim can be robbed, abducted, sexually assaulted, and even killed. Each year, about three hundred people are abducted during carjackings.

A carjacking can happen when the driver is getting into or out of his or her car. It can also happen when a car is stopped at a red light or stop sign. Carjacking is a dangerous crime because carjackers often threaten the driver and passengers with a weapon. Sometimes, the carjacker will force the driver and passengers out of the car so that he can steal it. Sometimes, he will drive away with the driver and passengers so that he can rob or harm them.

Carjackers may bump a car while driving to make the victim stop and get out. Never get out of the car. Motion to the driver to follow you to the nearest police station.

Protecting Yourself Against Carjackings

When returning to your parked car, look for strangers loitering nearby. If someone is loitering near your parked car, walk past it. Come back when the stranger has left. When you do approach your car, have your keys ready. Fumbling with your keys only gives a carjacker or abductor time to get close to you. Before getting into a parked car, check that no one is hiding in the backseat or on the floor.

While driving your car, keep the doors locked and windows shut. This prevents anyone from getting inside. Beware of people approaching your car when you are stopped at a red light or stop sign. If someone suspicious approaches your car, drive away at a safe speed. Some carjackers pretend that they want to ask you directions or sell you something so that they can get close enough to open your car door.

If another car bumps yours while you are driving, do not get out of the car. Signal the other driver to follow you. Then drive to the nearest police station or a busy, well-lit store, restaurant, or gas station. You can exchange insurance information there. Some carjackers purposely cause minor accidents in secluded areas to lure drivers from their cars.

Avoid driving in dangerous neighborhoods if there is another route available.

When Your Car Breaks Down

If your car breaks down or runs out of gas on the highway, you are vulnerable to criminals. Many stranded motorists have been attacked or robbed by strangers after their cars have broken down. These strangers will offer to help repair the car or drive the motorist to a gas station. But these offers are tricks to get the motorist out of the car, making it easier for the motorist to be robbed or harmed.

Car breakdowns can often be prevented. Make sure that your car has enough gasoline before leaving on any trip, no matter how close the destination may be. Keep the car in good repair so that the chances of it breaking down are small.

Sometimes, however, even the most reliable car will break down. If your car breaks down on the highway, stay inside, lock the doors, and shut the windows. Wait until a police car comes by and flag it down. If another motorist stops and offers to help, open the window just far enough to ask him to call a tow truck for you. Do not get out of the car, even if he claims he can fix your problem.

Always keep a list of emergency numbers in the car. If you have a cell phone, bring it everywhere you go and keep it fully charged. If you do not have a cell phone, look into buying or subscribing to a cell phone service that offers emergency calls only. This type of service is usually cheaper than paying for unlimited usage. If you get into trouble, you can call your parents or a tow truck without leaving your car and you will not have to wait for a police car to come by.

Sometimes, you may pass by other drivers who are having car problems. Never stop and offer assistance to stranded motorists. Criminals sometimes pretend that their cars have broken down to lure other motorists into getting out of their cars.

If You Get Lost

As often as you can, avoid driving through areas you're unfamiliar with. If you get lost, don't drive around aimlessly; this makes you an easier target. Drive to a busy place to pull over and use your cell phone. If you don't have a cell phone, use a phone inside a store or gas station. If you get out of your car to ask for directions or to use the phone, always lock your doors, no matter how brief you think your call or conversation may be.

The Danger of Hitchhiking

Some teenagers think that hitchhiking is an adventurous, thrilling thing to do or an easy way to get around. However, countless crimes have been committed against hitchhikers by the motorists who have picked them up. Hitchhiking can be very unsafe for both the hitchhiker and the motorist. Hitchhiking is a very dangerous activity that has led to the murder, rape, and robbery of many teenagers.

Hitchhiking is risky because it puts you in a car alone with a stranger—and the stranger is driving the car and can take you wherever he wants to go. You are entrusting your life to someone you don't know. This person could be a criminal—a thief, a rapist, or a murderer. The danger is the same whether someone picks you up or you pick someone else up.

Simply put, hitchhiking is too dangerous a way to get around. If you cannot drive or get a ride, take a bus or subway or walk. All these methods of transportation are safer than hitchhiking.

five

HOW CAN YOU USE THE INTERNET SAFELY?

Today, an ever-increasing number of teenagers are logging on to the Internet. You may go online to get help with homework or school projects, play games, or talk with others about common interests. However, online predators are always lurking, waiting for the opportunity to communicate with children and teenagers. Teenagers are especially at risk because they are more likely to participate in online discussions about relationships and sexual activity. According to a 2009 Cox Communications Teen Online and Wireless Safety Survey conducted in partnership with the National Center for Missing and Exploited Children, 72 percent of teens have a social networking profile, and nearly half of those teens have a public profile viewable by anyone.

Avoid giving out personal information over the Internet, and remember that someone may not be telling you the truth about themselves, so you need to be on your guard.

According to the U.S. Department of Justice's *Highlights of the Youth Internet Survey*, one in five children from the ages of ten to seventeen receive unwanted sexual solicitations online.

The way potential abductors communicate with teenagers is by tricking or lying to them. A thirty-year-old abductor or child molester may log on to the Internet and pretend to be a teenager himself. This way, he can trick teens into trusting him. The abductor can then convince a teen to have a face-to-face meeting with him.

When online, take the following precautions:

• Never give out any personal information, such as your home address, age, telephone number or cell phone number, school name and location, or places where you frequently go.

• Never send someone your picture or a video of yourself, or videos of friends, over the Internet.

• If you are going to get together with someone you met online, make sure that the meeting place is in a public area with many people around. Take someone else with you, and let your parents or friends know about the meeting. Never agree to a meeting at the stranger's home, your own home, or in a secluded spot.

• Be careful about claims that sound too good to be true. Offers of jobs or free products should be a warning signal, especially if they involve going to someone's home.

• Keep in mind that no matter how friendly or nice a person may seem—or what he tells you about himself—

he may not be telling the truth. You can't hear or see him, and you really don't know him, so there's no reason to trust him.

The Internet is a fun and exciting way to learn new things and meet new people. It may also be an essential tool used for schoolwork. Most of the people you meet online may be there for the same reasons, and most of them mean you no harm. But you need to keep in mind that there are individuals who have other intentions. Always use precautions to keep yourself and others safe.

10 Great Questions to Ask a Guidance Counselor

1 How can teens protect themselves from a kidnapper when in a park?

2 Why do abductors use shopping malls and parking lots for finding young victims?

3 How can teens stay safe on the Internet?

4 How can young people tell the difference between a friendly stranger and one who has evil intentions?

5 What should you do at home when a stranger comes to the door asking for help?

6 How can you get home safely after dark?

7 What should you do if your car breaks down and you don't have a cell phone?

8 What should you do if someone tries to abduct you by force while walking down the street?

9 How can you protect your little sister or brother from being kidnapped by a stranger who says there is an emergency at home?

10 How can you find out if there is a child molester living in your neighborhood?

SIX

WHAT IS SOCIETY DOING ABOUT ABDUCTION?

Policy makers and law enforcement personnel are constantly attempting to address the broader problem of missing children. Children who are away from the care of their parents, for whatever reason, are vulnerable to dangerous situations. Law enforcement personnel and the public want to return these children to their parents or guardians as soon as possible.

Studies, such as NISMART-2, use statistical data to show officials the facts about abduction. With this data, officials can design programs to protect American youth and go after the perpetrators of abduction. Internet safety hotlines, twenty-four-hour hotlines for reporting missing children, and tips to prevent abduction for parents and children are just some of the things that have been put into effect. Below are recent steps policy makers have taken to protect children in the United States.

In 2001, Megan Kanka's family watch the acting governor of New Jersey sign a law creating an Internet registry of sex offenders in the state. It's called Megan's Law, after the seven-year-old who was abducted, raped, and murdered in 1994.

Megan's Law

In 1996, the U.S. Congress passed a new law designed to help protect young people from sexual predators. Megan's Law orders local police officials to inform a neighborhood when a convicted child molester moves into the community.

This law was named after Megan Kanka, a seven-year-old girl from New Jersey who was abducted, raped, and murdered in 1994. Megan was killed by a neighbor who was a convicted child molester. Neither Megan, her parents, or anyone else in the neighborhood were aware of the man's background. While Megan's Law and other laws strive to protect young people from dangerous criminals, you also need to take safety measures to protect yourself and others.

AMBER Alert

The AMBER Alert system, started in 1996, is an early-warning system that teams local broadcasters, police, and state transportation officials together to help track down abductors and their victims. AMBER stands for America's Missing: Broadcast Emergency Response. It is named after nine-year-old Amber Hagerman, who was abducted while riding her bicycle in Arlington, Texas, and then murdered.

Once law enforcement has determined that a child has been abducted and the case meets certain criteria, officials interrupt radio and television programming to issue the AMBER Alert. The alert that a child is missing can also be seen on highway signs and can be sent over the Internet or to cell phones. All fifty states have an AMBER Alert system, and the Department of Justice is working toward a nationwide network. According to the AMBER Alert Web site, this program has been effective in saving the lives of more than two hundred children in the United States.

Child Abduction Response Team (CART)

The Child Abduction Response Team (CART) system, part of the Department of Justice, was started in 2005. These teams quickly

Drivers in Georgia are alerted by a sign to be on the lookout for a vehicle being driven by an abductor. AMBER Alert uses highway signs, the Internet, and cell phones to warn the public about missing children.

respond to abduction cases and other cases of missing children, such as runaways under the age of eighteen.

This system helps ensure that there are trained experts in the field of child abduction involved in an investigation. A Child Abduction Response Team will use many different officials, including law enforcement investigators, forensic experts, AMBER Alert coordinators, and search-and-rescue professionals. Many states, through various law enforcement agencies, offer training programs for CART. These teams are usually involved in the immediate response to an abducted child report. Typical training includes testimonials from the family members of abducted children, legal issues, investigative procedures, communications issues, and the various resources available in the communities. Many states also conduct joint training exercises that involve hundreds of first responders who take part in the live drill.

bribery The act of doing favors for or giving gifts to a person in order to influence his or her decisions.

carjacking The theft of a car using force or threats against the driver.

hitchhiking Going from place to place by getting free rides from passing cars.

impersonator A person pretending to be someone else.

indefinitely Having no time limit.

loitering Staying in an area for no obvious reason.

molest To physically force sexual advances upon another.

pedophile An adult who engages in sexual activities with children or teenagers.

pornography Materials, such as books or videos, that show sexual activity to excite the viewer sexually.

rapist A person who has sex with someone without his or her consent, often through the use of threats or force.

recreation Play or amusement.

serial killer A person who kills several people using similar patterns or methods over a period of time.

sexual predator A person who attacks others, usually to rape or molest them.

stereotypical kidnapping As defined by the U.S. Department of Justice, an abduction by a stranger or slight acquaintance involving a child who is transported 50 miles (80.5 km) or more, detained overnight, held for ransom or with the intention of keeping the child permanently, or killed.

vulnerable Open to attack or injury.

Amber Alert
Office of Justice Programs
U.S. Department of Justice
810 Seventh Street NW
Washington, DC 20531
(202) 307 0703
Web site: http://www.amberalert.gov
This is the official Amber Alert Web site from the U.S.
 Department of Justice's Office of Justice Programs. The
 Web site explains how an Amber Alert works. Information
 on Child Abduction Response Teams and tips for parents,
 children, and teens are also available.

Crimes Against Children (CAC)
Federal Bureau of Investigation
935 Pennsylvania Avenue NW
Washington, DC 20535-0001
(202) 324-3000
Web site: http://www.fbi.gov/hq/cid/cac/crimesmain.htm
The CAC program provides an efficient response to all
 crimes reported against children.

Ministry of Community Safety & Correctional Services
EMO A.R.E.S.
77 Wellesley Street West, Box 222

Toronto, ON M7A 1N3

Canada

(416) 628-6592

Web site: http://www.emoares.org

EMO A.R.E.S., in conjunction with Ontario A.R.E.S., operates a
series of networks utilizing a wide range of telecommunica-
tions equipment and technology in the interest of public
safety and service.

National Center for Missing and Exploited Children (NCMEC)

Charles B. Wang International Children's Building

699 Prince Street

Alexandria, VA 22314-3174

Hotline: 800-THE-LOST (800-843-5678)

Web site: http://www.missingkids.com

The NCMEC provides services to families and law enforcement
in the prevention of abducted, endangered, and exploited
children. These services include the distribution of photos of
missing children worldwide and a CyberTipline where
people can report Internet-related crimes against children.

National Runaway Switchboard

3080 North Lincoln Avenue

Chicago, IL 60657

(800) 786-2929

Web site: http://www.1800runaway.org

This organization is dedicated to keeping runaways in the
United States safe and off the streets. Its hotline is available
twenty-four hours a day and provides crisis counseling and
information about community resources.

Nation's Missing Children Organization (NMCO)

P.O. Box 19

Bentonville, AR

Hotline: (800) 690-FIND (3463)

Web site: http://www.theyaremissed.org/ncma/nmco.php

The NMCO is a nonprofit organization that assists law enforcement officials and families with finding missing children. It
provides searching assistance, child safety and ID awareness
programs, and distributes information nationwide regarding
the details of a missing child.

NetSmartz Workshop

Web site: http://www.netsmartz.org/Teens

This educational Web site, created by the National Center for
Missing and Exploited Children, teaches kids and teens all
about online safety. The section for teens offers information
on cyberbullying, real-life stories of teens who have been the
victims of Internet exploitation, and recent news articles on
teens' online experiences.

Our Missing Children

c/o National Missing Children Service

Royal Canadian Mounted Police

1200 Vanier Parkway

Ottawa, ON K1A 0R2

Canada

(613) 993-1525

Web site: http://www.rcmp-grc.gc.ca/omc-ned

The objective of this agency is to provide an investigative
assistance service to all Canadian and foreign police

agencies and to assist police and searching agencies to locate, recover and return missing children and youth to their proper guardian.

Web Sites

Due to the changing nature of Internet links, Rosen Publishing has developed an online list of Web sites related to the subject of this book. This site is updated regularly. Please use this link to access the list:

http://www.rosenlinks.com/faq/knap

For Further Reading

Burns, Jan. *Kidnapping* (Crime Scene Investigations).
Farmington Hills, MI: Lucent, 2007.

Colt, James P. *Cyberpredators* (Cybersafety). New York, NY:
Chelsea House Publishers, 2011.

Cooney, Caroline B. *Face on the Milk Carton*. New York,
NY: Bantam Books, 1990.

Dingwell, Heath, Robert N. Golden, and Fred L. Peterson.
The Truth About the Internet and Online Predators. New
York, NY: Facts On File, 2011.

Frangos, Amber. *No Child Is Safe from Internet Crime*.
Thonotossasa, FL: DDR Publications, 2005.

Gallop-Goodman, Gerda. *Crimes Against Women* (Crime,
Justice & Punishment). New York, NY: Chelsea House
Publishers, 2002.

Gerdes, Louise I., and Murray Gell-Mann. *Child Abuse*
(Opposing Viewpoints). Farmington Hills, MI:
Greenhaven Press, 2003.

Hansen, Chris. *To Catch a Predator: Protecting Your Kids
from Online Enemies Already in Your Home*. New York,
NY: Dutton, 2007.

Kehret, Peg. *ABDUCTION!* New York, NY: Dutton Books, 2004.

Mitchard, Jacquelyn. *Now You See Her*. New York, NY:
HarperTeen, 2007.

Mooney, Carla. *Online Predators* (Issues in the Digital Age).
San Diego, CA: ReferencePoint Press, 2011.

O'Brien, Susan. *Child Abduction and Kidnapping* (Criminal Investigations). New York, NY: Chelsea House Publishers, 2008.

Rogers, Vanessa. *Cyberbullying: Activities to Help Children and Teens to Stay Safe in a Texting, Twittering, Social Networking World*. London, England: Jessica Kingsley Publishers, 2010.

Salter, Anna C. *Predators: Pedophiles, Rapists, and Other Sex Offenders*. New York, NY: Basic Books, 2004.

Sommers, Michael A. *Dangers of Online Predators*. New York, NY: Rosen Publishing Group, 2008.

Willard, Nancy E. *Cyber-Safe Kids, Cyber-Savvy Teens: Helping Young People Learn to Use the Internet Safely and Responsibly*. San Francisco, CA: Jossey-Bass, 2007.

Willis, Laurie. *Sexual Predators* (Social Issues Firsthand). Farmington Hills, MI: Greenhaven Press, 2008.

Index

A

abduction
  how it is carried out, 15–22, 40, 47
  long-term effects, 10
  types of, 6–10
alert attitude, as defense, 37–39
AMBER Alert, 52, 54
automobile safety, 13, 31–32, 41–43

B

babysitting, 26–28
bribes, 10, 17–19

C

car breakdowns, 42–43, 49
carjackings, 40–42
Child Abduction Response Team (CART), 52–54
child pornography, 9
code words, 40
courtesy patrol, 32
Crime of Family Abduction: A Child's and Parent's Perspective, 12

D

defense spray, 37

F

family abductions, 6, 9–10, 12
family emergency, as lure for victims, 19, 49

flirting, 16
following victims home, 29

G

guidance counselor, questions to ask a, 49

H

handheld alarm, 37
help, asking for to lure victims, 17, 49
hitchhiking, 12, 44
human trafficking, 10

I

ID, 25
impersonation, 19–20, 23–25
Internet safety, 45–48, 49

J

job offers, as lure for victims, 18–19, 47
Juvenile Offenders and Victims 2006 National Report, 4

K

Kanka, Megan, 51

L

license plate numbers, 36, 37
lost, what to do if you get, 43

M

Megan's Law, 51–52

murder, 4, 5, 10, 23, 25, 31, 40, 44, 51, 52

N

National Center for Missing and Exploited Children, 45
noise, as defense against abduction, 22, 29, 36, 37, 39–40
nonfamily abductions, 6–8, 12

O

Office of Juvenile Justice and Delinquency Prevention, 12

P

parks, 36, 49
pay telephones, 39, 43
pedophiles, 8, 49, 51
phone calls, as tactic to enter homes, 26
police officers, impersonating, 19–20
postal workers, impersonating, 25
prostitution, 10
public places, avoiding abduction in, 37–40
  jogging and cycling, 36–37
  malls and stores, 30, 32, 33–34, 49
  parking lots, 30–33, 49
  the street, 34–36, 49

R

ransom, 6
rape, 5, 8, 10–11, 16, 23, 25, 31, 32, 40, 44, 51

Rape, Abuse and Incest National Network, 16
repairmen, impersonating, 24–25
rides, offered to lure victims, 17, 44
robbery, 10, 23, 25, 31, 40, 42, 44
runaways, 10, 54

S

safety hotlines, 50
Second National Incidence Studies of Missing, Abducted, Runaway, and Thrownaway Children (NISMART-2), 6–8, 9, 50
security guards, 32, 33
serial killers, 10
signature collection, as abductor's ploy, 25

T

threats, 6, 20, 40

U

U.S. Department of Justice (DOJ), 4, 6, 8, 10, 47, 52

V

vans, 37, 39
violence, to capture victims, 6, 12, 20–22, 40

W

weapons, 12, 22

About the Authors

Randy Shattuck is a writer who lives in Edina, Minnesota.

Kristina Lundblad has written several books for young adults. A former publishing professional, Lundblad lives in New York.

Photo Credits

Cover Shutterstock.com; p. 5 Sarasota County Sheriff's Office via Getty Images; pp. 7, 51 © AP Images; p. 11 Tim Boyle/Getty Images; p. 15 Noel Hendrickson/Digital Vision/Thinkstock.com; p. 18 © Angela Hampton Picture Library/Alamy; p. 21 Robert Nickelsberg/Getty Images; p. 24 Ed Honowitz/Stone/Getty Images; p. 27 © www.istockphoto.com/Joanne Green; p. 28 David Young-Wolff/Stone/Getty Images; p. 31 © www.istockphoto.com/parema; p. 33 Jessie Jean/Taxi/Getty Images; p. 35 iStockphoto/Thinkstock.com; p. 38 Jupiterimages/Comstock/Thinkstock.com; p. 41 Hemera/Thinkstock.com; p. 46 © Augusta Chronicle/ZUMAPRESS.com; p. 53 Erik S. Lesser/Getty Images.

Editor: Kathy Campbell; Photo Researcher: Amy Feinberg